Hire Smarter, Sell More!

Using Talent Analytics to Discover Sales Rainmakers
and Avoid Toxic Troublemakers

C. Lee Smith

THiNKaha®

An Actionable Sales Journal

E-mail: info@thinkaha.com
20660 Stevens Creek Blvd., Suite 210
Cupertino, CA 95014

Please go to
https://aha.pub/HireSmarterSellMore
to read this AHAbook and to share the
individual AHAmessages that resonate with you.

Published by THiNKaha®
20660 Stevens Creek Blvd., Suite 210,
Cupertino, CA 95014
https://thinkaha.com
E-mail: **info@thinkaha.com**

First Printing: April 2020
Hardcover ISBN: 978-1-61699-357-3   1-61699-357-X
Paperback ISBN: 978-1-61699-356-6   1-61699-356-1
eBook ISBN: 978-1-61699-355-9   1-61699-355-3
Place of Publication: Silicon Valley, California, USA
Paperback Library of Congress Number: 2020904224

Trademarks

All terms mentioned in this book that are known to be trademarks or service marks have been appropriately capitalized. Neither THiNKaha, nor any of its imprints, can attest to the accuracy of this information. Use of a term in this book should not be regarded as affecting the validity of any trademark or service mark.

Warning and Disclaimer

Every effort has been made to make this book as complete and as accurate as possible. The information provided is on an "as is" basis. The author(s), publisher, and their agents assume no responsibility for errors or omissions. Nor do they assume liability or responsibility to any person or entity with respect to any loss or damages arising from the use of information contained herein.

PROFILE YOURSELF FOR FREE!

What does your profile look like?
Visit https://www.salesfuel.com/hire-book, and use your LinkedIn account to get a free sales hiring profile. You'll also be added to my email list of free sales and management insights.

Dedication

I dedicate this book to my wife, Kelly, and my two sons, Jason and Justin. My family has always been there to help celebrate the rainmakers and support me when dealing with my handful of toxic mistakes. They know first-hand that it hasn't always been easy.

I also dedicate this book to my work family at SalesFuel, an extraordinary group of loyal and talented people who really are like my second family.

Acknowledgements

Thank you to:

Jeffrey Gitomer, author of four *New York Times* bestselling books on sales, including *The Little Red Book of Sales*, and my professional mentor. Ever since I became one of his first Certified Advisors in 2013, he's been after me to write this book.

Steve Sisler, my partner in behavioral analytics and the CEO of Behavioral Resource Group. Our collaboration led to the science behind the "13 Types of Toxic Salespeople" in the back of this book.

Roy E. White, that one special teacher from high school who was like a second father to me. The scientific method is still a key part of everything I do in business today.

Cyndy Goldsworthy, another special teacher from high school who also went the extra mile. This may not be a literary masterpiece, but it will help many people, like you helped me.

The late Norman Shub, my executive coach who opened my eyes to the importance of empathy, soft skills, and what I needed to become even more successful in the years ahead.

My late father, who instilled core values and drove me to become who I am today in the best way he knew how.

Kathy Crosett, for spearheading the primary research referenced inside, and Tyler Welsh for designing the graphics.

And lastly, thank you to all the rainmakers and toxic people I've worked with. In addition to all the research, thirty-five years of experience have gone into this book.

How to Read a THiNKaha® Book
A Note from the Publisher

The AHAthat/THiNKaha series is the CliffsNotes of the 21st century. These books are contextual in nature. Although the actual words won't change, their meaning will every time you read one as your context will change. Be ready, you will experience your own AHA moments as you read the AHA messages™ in this book. They are designed to be stand-alone actionable messages that will help you think about a project you're working on, an event, a sales deal, a personal issue, etc., differently. As you read this book, please think about the following:

1. It should only take 15–20 minutes to read this book the first time out. When you're reading, write in the underlined area one to three action items that resonate with you.
2. Mark your calendar to re-read this book again in 30 days.
3. Repeat step #1 and mark one to three more AHA messages that resonate. They will most likely be different than the first time. BTW: this is also a great time to reflect on the AHA messages that resonated with you during your last reading.

After reading a THiNKaha book, marking your AHA messages, re-reading it, and marking more AHA messages, you'll begin to see how these books contextually apply to you. AHAthat/THiNKaha books advocate for continuous, lifelong learning. They will help you transform your AHAs into actionable items with tangible results until you no longer have to say AHA to these moments—they'll become part of your daily practice as you continue to grow and learn.

Mitchell Levy, Global Credibility Expert
publisher@thinkaha.com

THiNKaha®

Contents

Introduction

"The smartest business decision you can make is to hire qualified people. Bringing the right people on board saves you thousands, and your business will run smoothly and efficiently. [But] hiring the wrong person is the most costly mistake you can make."

—Brian Tracy
Author of *The Psychology of Selling* and eighty other business success books
Featured guest on Episode 5 of the *Manage Smarter* podcast

It's an all-too-common tale, told across just about every sales department around the world: The newest salesperson on the team has strong credentials and crushed it during the interview. But now that they're hired, they can't sell a thing! Worse, other salespeople on the team are unhappy for some reason, and their performance is slipping.

Every new job opening is an opportunity to make your sales team better or worse. In fact, the top responsibility of a sales manager is not to make numbers. It's to build, develop, and motivate a high-performing sales team (so they can make the numbers).

The best-case scenario is that you'll recruit and hire a "rainmaker," an A player who outperforms their competition and everyone else on your current team. When you know the traits that rainmakers possess—and if your candidate possesses them as well—you'll have a much greater chance of adding this kind of potential to your team. Even if you come up short, you're much more likely to hire good salespeople.

The worst-case scenario is not hiring someone who can't sell. It's hiring someone who is cancerous to your sales team. Just about all of us have horror stories of what it was like to work with (or work for) these divisive and destructive personalities. You need to know what to look for, the tricks that toxic salespeople use to get hired, and how to spot them, so you can avoid derailing your sales team.

During my thirty-five years in sales management, I've had the joy of hiring many rainmakers. I've also had the pain of hiring a handful of toxic employees. My mission is to give you the insight needed to protect yourself from the worst-case scenario, while preparing you for the success of making a great hire.

The book shares four years of research from my team at SalesFuel. We have conducted three exclusive studies, surveying hundreds of sales managers, salespeople and buyers about hiring practices and what they each believe makes up a desirable salesperson.

In collaboration with our partners at Behavioral Resources Group, we have also studied the key psychological, behavioral and motivational characteristics of each group using data from some of largest sales teams in the world.

The good news is while hiring salespeople may always seem like a gamble, talent analytics can help stack the deck in your favor.

Talent analytics are data-based insights into the behaviors, attitudes, personality traits, and sales aptitude of your candidate pool that enable you to make better hiring decisions.

The pages that follow will show sales managers and recruiters what metrics to use—along with common-sense best practices— that will enable you to identify potential rainmakers and avoid toxic hiring mistakes.

Hire smarter, sell more. Start now.

WHY MINDSET MATTERS

Sales Rainmakers		Toxic Troublemakers
Strong	**Values/ Beliefs**	Strong, but Limiting
Driven by Desire and ROI	**Motivation**	Controlled by Need
Focused, Adaptive, Constructive, Serves Others	**Behavior**	Divisive, Self-serving and/or Dysfunctional
Net Gain	**Results**	Net Loss

Mindset is the key leading indicator of the salesperson you're going to get once you hire them. Results are not only financial, but also the their impact on others on your team.

Share the AHA messages from this book socially by going to
https://aha.pub/HireSmarterSellMore.

Section I

The Danger of Hiring a Toxic Salesperson

Four percent of the adult population are sociopaths. Nearly 1 in 12 candidates are likely to become toxic employees if/when the situation triggers them. Adding a toxic salesperson to the team can mean downfall. They can cause lost time and opportunity, both of which are crucial to sales success.

Toxic salespeople affect everyone around them: their sales managers, their coworkers, and, especially, their customers! This section discusses the most important reasons that a sales manager should be mindful about avoiding hiring toxic salespeople.

Scan the QR code or use this link to watch the section videos:
https://aha.pub/HireSmarterSellMoreSVs

1

The top responsibility of a sales manager is not to make numbers. It's to build, develop, and motivate a high-performing sales team. The biggest detriment to this mission is adding toxicity to the team. #HireSmarter

_____

_____

_____

2

It takes an average of 7 months to offboard a poorly performing or toxic salesperson. https://salesfuel.com/voice-of-the-sales-manager/ #HireSmarter

_____

_____

_____

3

2/3 of salespeople have reported working with a toxic co-worker or working for a toxic manager. How does it usually end? Either dismissal of the toxic employee or departure of the affected salespeople. #HireSmarter @SalesFuel

_____

_____

4

The only thing worse than making a bad hire is making a toxic hire. Bad salespeople have low-performance levels. Toxic salespeople lower the performance of others. #HireSmarter

_____

_____

_____

5

Hiring a toxic salesperson can cost companies 133-213% of their annual compensation. —Center for American Progress, Salary.com, and BIA Advisory Services via https://aha.pub/CLeeSmith #AvoidToxicity #HireSmarter

_____

_____

_____

6

The true cost of hiring a toxic salesperson includes lost time and opportunity. #HireSmarter

_____

_____

_____

7

If you think hiring a top-tier salesperson is expensive, wait until you hire a toxic one. #HireSmarter

_____

_____

_____

8

Toxicity can come in many forms. Sales managers should know and understand how toxic salespeople behave, and spot these behaviors before hiring. #HireSmarter

_____

_____

_____

9

Toxic employees often have two or more of these characteristics in common: low accountability, self-importance, entitlement, histrionics, lack of empathy, anti-social behavior, low self-esteem, and untrustworthiness. #HireSmarter

_____

_____

10

There are 13 types of toxic salespeople. Knowing each type can help sales managers and recruiters easily spot a toxic hire. #HireSmarter https://info.salesfuel.com/13typestoxicityebook

_____

_____

_____

11

Symptoms of sales team toxicity: stress, anger, tension that carries over to home life, sadness, dread coming to work, disengagement, walking on eggshells, higher absentee rates, higher turnover, and even legal action. #HireSmarter @SalesFuel

_____

_____

_____

12

Toxic salespeople drain time, energy, and positivity that should be used for increasing revenue. #HireSmarter

_____

_____

_____

13

Toxic salespeople also waste the time of their sales managers, causing them to be mediators and internal fire extinguishers, which cheats better salespeople of valuable coaching and development. #HireSmarter

_____

_____

_____

14

Damage from a toxic salesperson is measured in drama and dollars. #AvoidToxicity #HireSmarter

_____

_____

_____

15

The effects of hiring a toxic salesperson last long after they're gone. It can take months before the culture fully returns to what it was. Prevention is better than cure. #HireSmarter

_____

_____

_____

16

If there are gains in hiring toxic yet performing salespeople, those will easily be offset by the decrease in the sales team's energy over time. #HireSmarter

_____

_____

_____

17

The two happiest days of having a toxic employee on your sales team are their first day of work and their last. #HireSmarter

_____

_____

_____

THE SALES HIRING FUNNEL

Attract

Screen

Profile

Interview

Audition

Offer

Don't let them tell you that they can do the job. Make them prove it with an Audition stage. This gives rainmakers a chance to shine and toxic candidates another chance to expose themselves.

Share the AHA messages from this book socially by going to
https://aha.pub/HireSmarterSellMore.

Section II

How Toxic Salespeople Get Hired and How to Avoid Them

Many sales managers have had the experience of hiring salespeople who were great during the interview and kicked ass in their sales test but caused toxic problems as soon as they got on the team.

This section goes over how the thirteen types of toxic salespeople behave toward others. It discusses common reasons that toxic salespeople get hired and dives into the loopholes that sales managers or recruiters may unconsciously have in their hiring process and mindset.

More details about toxic personality types and real-world stories of the damage they cause can be found in the Appendix of this book.

When sales managers and recruiters know how toxic salespeople get hired, it's easier to come up with plans to avoid them. If you never hire them, you'll never have to fire them—which is often a tedious process laden with landmines.

Scan the QR code or use this link to watch
the section videos:
https://aha.pub/HireSmarterSellMoreSVs

18

Every open position is an opportunity to improve a sales team. But be careful! Nearly 1 in 12 candidates have the tendency to bring toxicity to the workplace. #HireSmarter

_____

_____

_____

19

35% of sales managers say that it's harder to hire good salespeople than it was a year ago. The bigger problem is that it's easy to hire bad ones. https://salesfuel.com/voice-of-the-sales-manager/ #HireSmarter

_____

_____

_____

20

Toxic salespeople can be experienced interviewees (for a reason). They may know most of the standard interview questions that a recruiter may ask. #HireSmarter

_____

_____

_____

21

Most toxic salespeople can turn on the charm during the interview. However, once they get hired, sales managers may never see that performance again. #HireSmarter

_____

_____

_____

22

Toxic salespeople know how to: 1) artfully talk about their successes and 2) dance around questions about things they weren't successful at. #HireSmarter

_____

_____

_____

23

To avoid hiring toxic salespeople, focus interview questions on candidate mindset, beliefs, and sales methodology — not on job history and standard interview questions. #HireSmarter

_____

_____

_____

24

Use your interview time wisely. Sales managers and recruiters should not allow the interview to become a conversation about metrics that are irrelevant to the sales position. #HireSmarter

_____

_____

_____

25

Make sure they know YOUR stuff, not just their stuff. If pre-hire conversations are focused on them, instead of what they can do for you, you're either recruiting or they're giving you clues about their future conduct.
#HireSmarter

_____

_____

_____

26

Toxic salespeople often revise their employment history in order to hide something from a potential employer.
#HireSmarter

_____

_____

_____

27

LinkedIn profiles can be a work of fiction. In fact, there is a cottage industry of people who do exactly that! You can't rely on them for employment history. #HireSmarter

_____

_____

_____

28

Freelance work or operating their own sales consultancy businesses are tactics that toxic salespeople use on their employment history to cover up terminations and bridge gaps. #HireSmarter

_____

_____

_____

29

Sales managers and recruiters should make sales candidates sign a tried-but-true employment application that ensures they're providing true and accurate data about themselves.

_____

_____

_____

30

Always assume a sales candidate is stretching the truth to some degree. Toxic candidates will bristle when you ask probing questions that could expose inconsistencies in their story. #HireSmarter

_____

_____

_____

31

Trust but verify! For example, if a sales candidate is bragging about their contact list, get the names and numbers for five of their strongest contacts. Then contact them! #HireSmarter

_____

_____

_____

32

No shortcuts! Be sure to contact former employers, but don't just listen to WHAT they say. The information you're looking for could be in HOW they say it. #HireSmarter

_____

_____

_____

33

What former employers can tell you is limited. Use LinkedIn to reach out to former colleagues of the candidate — even better if the colleague no longer works for the former employer. #HireSmarter

_____

_____

_____

34

Listen well! Toxic salespeople are overly focused on themselves and not focused enough on serving others. They won't be able to help customers achieve their goals. #HireSmarter

_____

_____

_____

35

Involve people like the waiter at lunch, the receptionist, or even the intern in your hiring process. Toxic salespeople often show their true colors to people whom they think are there to "serve" them. #HireSmarter

_____

_____

_____

36

Don't be in a hurry to fill an open position. When sales managers and recruiters get pressured and rushed into hiring salespeople, they are less likely to notice if a salesperson is toxic. #HireSmarter

_____

_____

_____

37

Never settle! Hiring fatigue can cause sales managers and recruiters to tender an offer to a salesperson who will likely 1. deliver poor/marginal performance and/or 2. bring toxicity into the workplace. #HireSmarter

_____

_____

_____

38

Make the hiring process lengthy. Anyone can be nice for an hour. A toxic salesperson is more likely to display their impatience or complain about how long the hiring process is. #HireSmarter

_____

_____

_____

39

Give all sales candidates a clearly defined task with a deadline. Include broken links or missing info. Toxic salespeople will complain about the mistakes as an excuse for their less-than-stellar results. #HireSmarter

_____

_____

_____

40

Use auditions to test a sales candidate's talent and agility. A strong candidate will find a way to overcome adversity and rise to the challenge, while a toxic candidate will complain. #HireSmarter

_____

_____

_____

41

Beware the siren's song. An audition that only consists of a delivering a stage performance or presentation is often right in the toxic salesperson's wheelhouse. #HireSmarter

_____

_____

_____

42

Double-check to make sure the criminal background check has not been overlooked - a recipe for disaster. Be sure to follow applicable laws in doing so. Toxic candidates won't volunteer this info no matter how you ask the question. #HIreSmarter

---

43

For sales managers, it's not A-B-C, but A-B-R: always be recruiting. Starting with an empty pipeline can lead to desperation and bad decisions when an opening unexpectedly pops up. #HireSmarter

---

44

Sales managers and recruiters need to look for reasons not to hire a salesperson just as much as they need to look for the opposite. You're hiring, not recruiting. #HireSmarter

_____

_____

_____

45

Toxic salespeople are easy to find but damn difficult to get rid of. If you never hire them, you won't have to fire them. #HireSmarter

_____

_____

_____

THE FOUR FITS OF HIRING GREAT SALESPEOPLE

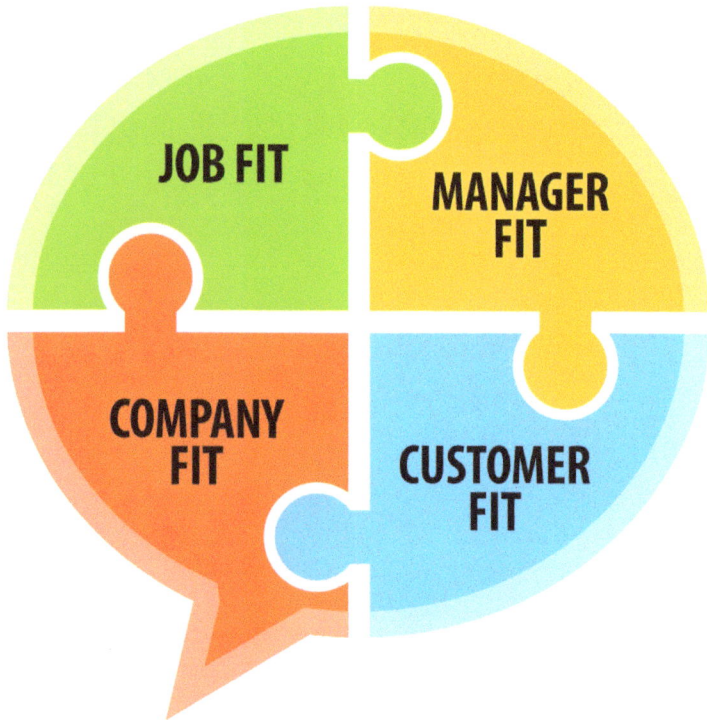

JOB FIT

MANAGER FIT

COMPANY FIT

CUSTOMER FIT

The Four Fits is not a rubric, it's a gauntlet.
A misfit in any area is a sign to keep looking.

Share the AHA messages from this book socially by going to
https://aha.pub/HireSmarterSellMore.

Section III

The Four "Fits" of Sales Rainmakers

Rainmakers have the courage to pursue bigger accounts. They close bigger deals that are instrumental to helping your sales team meet its assigned goals.

Sales managers and recruiters should always aspire to hire potential rainmakers. If you come up short, you still have hired someone with the potential to be a very good salesperson. However, if your goal is to hire a B player, and you come up short, you'll end up adding a C player to your team.

Sales managers and recruiters need to understand that there are certain conditions or "fits" in which sales rainmakers are hired. These are:

1. Job fit
2. Manager fit
3. Company fit
4. Customer fit

When a sales candidate has the core competencies to do the job well, they are worthy of your consideration. When they possess the values, motivation, and behavior needed to impress their sales manager, appeal to the target customers, and have a positive impact on your team culture, they will likely be an ideal finalist. Salespeople who fit all four of these aspects have a higher likelihood of becoming sales rainmakers.

Scan the QR code or use this link to watch
the section videos:
https://aha.pub/HireSmarterSellMoreSVs

46

There are four "fits" of sales rainmakers: 1) job fit, 2) manager fit, 3) company fit, and 4) customer fit. With this focus, sales managers are better equipped to hire rainmakers. #HireSmarter

_____

_____

_____

47

The "four fits" for sales candidates is not a rubric. It's a gauntlet. A bad fit in any of these should be an indication to keep looking. #HireSmarter

_____

_____

_____

48

A rainmaker can be just the tonic for what ails your sales team. Hire TONIC, not TOXIC. #HireSmarter

_____

_____

_____

49

Success breeds success. Rainmakers can make a huge impact on the sales team's attitude and performance. #HireSmarter

_____

_____

_____

50

Rainmakers have strong beliefs in: their company, their product line, their management, their supporting cast, their sales process, and most importantly, themselves. #HireSmarter

_____

_____

_____

51

A sales candidate who requests to trade commission and incentives for a higher base salary is NOT a rainmaker. Rainmakers are more likely to do the opposite. They believe in their ability to make money. #HireSmarter

_____

_____

_____

52

Rainmakers are crystal clear in their future direction. They'll often set goals higher for themselves than you will. They just won't tell you about it. #HireSmarter

_____

_____

_____

53

Job history tells you where they've been. Mindset tells you where they're going. #HireSmarter

_____

_____

_____

54

Match mindset to your open position, not just competencies. Successful new business hunters require a different mindset than account managers. Closers have a different mindset than SDRs. #JobFit #HireSmarter

_____

_____

_____

55

Never hire a banana to do a milkshake's job. —Clay Christensen via https://aha.pub/CLeeSmith https://hbr.org/podcast/2016/12/the-jobs-to-be-done-theory-of-innovation #JobFit #HireSmarter

_____

_____

_____

56

If salespeople need to be assertive for their job when they're not, they will spend a great deal of energy trying to be effective. This is often not sustainable. #JobFit #HireSmarter

_____

_____

_____

57

What sales managers commonly look for in a salesperson: 1) problem solving skills, 2) confidence, 3) optimism, 4) initiative, and 5) time management. https://salesfuel.com/voice-of-the-sales-manager/ #HireSmarter

_____

_____

_____

58

Undervalued traits that sales managers should look for in a salesperson: 1) curiosity, 2) courage, 3) resilience, 4) empathy, and 5) coachability. https://salesfuel.com/voice-of-the-sales-manager/ #HireSmarter

_____

_____

_____

59

Looking for a sales rainmaker? Determine if your candidate is positive, curious, resilient, empathetic, and persuasive; has business acumen; and makes good decisions. #HireSmarter

_____

_____

_____

60

Resilience is a key part of what sets rainmakers apart from other salespeople on the team. Are you hiring for resilience? #HireSmarter

_____

_____

_____

61

Salespeople who are not curious and weak at discovery are also usually weak at closing. Rainmakers know that knowledge gained through discovery gives them the leverage they'll need during the closing stage. #HireSmarter

_____

_____

_____

62

Typical salespeople do a needs analysis. Rainmakers focus on wants. They not only focus on the benefits of solving a problem, but they also determine the consequences of not solving the problem. #JobFit #HireSmarter

_____

_____

_____

63

Pushiness is the biggest turnoff that buyers have today about salespeople. Rainmakers know how to walk the fine line between being assertive enough to get to "yes" and pissing off the prospect. #HireSmarter

_____

_____

_____

64

Rainmakers are always prepared. They are comfortable talking about money and business challenges. They also know what they want to accomplish with every action. #HireSmarter

_____

_____

_____

65

Rainmakers don't just embrace change, they cause it. Change requires that a product, service, or idea eventually be sold. Look for agents of change when hiring. #HireSmarter

_____

_____

_____

66

Your product is not a solution. The solution is the effective USE of your product to solve problems or achieve goals. This understanding is the value rainmakers bring. Your customers can use Google and your website for everything else. #HireSmarter

_____

_____

_____

67

The sales manager is the one who will interact the most with the salesperson. They need to get along well and be in alignment to achieve their sales goals. #ManagerFit #HireSmarter

_____

_____

_____

68

Up to 50% of salespeople leave their jobs due to not having a good relationship with their sales managers. Make sure to consider #ManagerFit. #HireSmarter

_____

_____

_____

69

Sales managers can set up how successful a young salesperson is going to be, not only in that job but also for most of their professional career. #ManagerFit #HireSmarter

_____

_____

_____

70

To determine compatibility and potential tension, sales managers also need to be profiled. #ManagerFit #UseData

_____

_____

_____

71

It's not just the money. Sales managers and recruiters need to fit the salesperson to the culture of the company — its vision, mission, and values. #CompanyFit #HireSmarter

_____

_____

_____

72

Salespeople who get along with their coworkers and share the company's values not only perform well as an individual, but they also inspire and motivate others on the team to perform well. #Rainmakers #HireSmarter

_____

_____

_____

73

Rainmakers will be pursued by others promising greener pastures. Once you hire them, will they have enough reason to stay? #CompanyFit #HireSmarter

_____

_____

_____

74

While salespeople need to fit with the company culture, they also need to fit its target customers. #CustomerFit #HireSmarter

_____

_____

_____

75

Sales managers who have a cutthroat and competitive culture should avoid hiring somebody who's collaborative and just wants to get along with their coworkers. #CompanyFit #HireSmarter

_____

_____

_____

76

Likeability is determined by how much the customer believes the salesperson genuinely likes them and cares about them FIRST. #CustomerFit #HireSmarter

_____

_____

_____

77

Some customers look for salespeople who don't just care about their business. They also look for those who care about their wellbeing. #CustomerFit #HireSmarter

_____

_____

_____

78

Sales managers and recruiters need to ensure that they are hiring salespeople whom their target customers will like and relate to. This often increases their closing rate. #CustomerFit #HireSmarter

_____

_____

_____

79

If your ideal customer is a highly polished, well-educated executive who regularly works with powerful people — and your salesperson is not — they are unlikely to gain the trust needed to be a rainmaker. #CustomerFit #HireSmarter

_____

_____

80

If a recruiter hires a great salesperson but pairs them with the wrong sales manager, company, or customer base, everybody loses. #HireSmarter

_____

_____

_____

81

Past performance is not indicative of future success. A candidate's new job, company, sales manager, product line, and customer base will likely be different. They may also be different people now than they were then. #HireSmarter

_____

_____

_____

82

Hiring rainmakers takes time and involves asking the right questions. In order to spot potential rainmakers, sales managers need to prepare well for the sales hiring process. #HireSmarter

_____

_____

_____

83

Sales rainmakers are unleashed when they: 1) naturally fit the job, 2) are able to relate with their customers, 3) are paired up with the right sales manager, 4) and are in alignment with the team and company culture. #HireSmarter

_____

_____

_____

SIX ELEMENTS OF A CANDIDATE PROFILE

06 TOXICITY FLAGS

01 SALES TENDENCIES

02 WORK TENDENCIES

03 DECISION-MAKING TENDENCIES

04 MOTIVATIONAL TENDENCIES

05 BEHAVIORAL TENDENCIES

For selling complex, high tech or highly regulated products, include Industry Aptitude into the profile

The cost of doing a comprehensive profile of your candidates is minuscule compared to the cost a toxic employee or the revenue a rainmaker can bring.

Share the AHA messages from this book socially by going to
https://aha.pub/HireSmarterSellMore.

Section IV

Using Data as Another Set of Eyes in the Sales Hiring Process

Hiring salespeople is not an easy process—it's often a gamble. So, stack the deck in your favor! Sales managers and recruiters need to understand the importance of using analytics and assessments. These data can be another set of eyes that verifies that the candidate you saw in their interview is really who they purported to be.

Early on in the hiring process, sales managers and recruiters should profile their sales candidates. This will alert you to things you need to watch for: attitude, people skills (soft skills), behavior under stress, motivation, empathy, critical thinking, and of course, selling tendencies.

Sales managers and recruiters need to be aware that just having a gut instinct or a single basis of reference is not enough. You need to use all the data you've gathered, as these pieces of information can complete the puzzle. Using data as another set of eyes can greatly increase the chance of successfully hiring good salespeople—even rainmakers!

Scan the QR code or use this link to watch
the section videos:
https://aha.pub/HireSmarterSellMoreSVs

84

Sales managers need to understand and be mindful of what their biases are in the hiring process if they want to #HireSmarter. #UseData to do so.

_____

_____

_____

85

Is the candidate you saw during the hiring process really who they purported to be? #UseData as checks and balances against your intuition. If the data shows something different, dig deeper. #HireSmarter

_____

_____

_____

86

Profiling sales candidates before an interview can act as an early warning system, alerting sales managers on what to watch for during the hiring process. #HireSmarter

_____

_____

_____

87

Important: Profiles must be administered consistently to all candidates in accordance to EEOC guidelines, as well as local and federal employment law. #UseData #HireSmarter

_____

_____

_____

88

A comprehensive profile includes measurement of mindset, which includes their: 1) attitude, 2) belief system, 3) values, 4) decision-making process, and 5) compassion for other people. #UseData #HireSmarter

_____

_____

_____

89

Sales managers need to test a sales candidate's knowledge and acumen. But it's one thing to have sales and business knowledge, it's another thing to apply it. This is how value is provided to the buyer. #HireSmarter

_____

_____

_____

90

A comprehensive profile is not a single assessment or data source. It is using MULTIPLE data sources to determine where patterns emerge. This will give you greater confidence in deciding whom to interview and hire. #HireSmarter

---

91

Profiling sales candidates early on in the hiring process can help you avoid wasting time interviewing people who won't be a good fit for the position. #HireSmarter

---

92

The employer is the buyer. At the very least, do at least as much research on your candidates as you would when buying a car or home. #UseData #HireSmarter

_____

_____

_____

93

Having a good profile of the salesperson ready before the interview allows sales managers to prepare questions that point directly to negative tendencies that the salesperson may have, to catch them off guard. #HireSmarter

---

94

If a salesperson's profile indicates that they may be sensitive to criticism, ask them about a recent time when a manager unfairly gave them negative feedback. How did they deal with the criticism? #HireSmarter

95

If a salesperson's profile indicates that they may lack attention to detail, ask them to intricately describe the nicest car or outfit they've owned. #HireSmarter

_____

_____

_____

96

If a salesperson's profile indicates that they may be highly motivated by power and control, ask them about situations in which they would prefer to not be in charge. #HireSmarter

_____

_____

_____

97

If a salesperson's profile indicates that they may have delusions of grandeur, ask them if they consider themselves to be an expert and why. #HireSmarter

_____

_____

_____

98

@CyWakeman suggests asking, "Tell me about a time when you couldn't produce the results you promised." Candidates that use the word "I" repeatedly (instead of he/she/they) are more likely to be highly accountable, less likely to be toxic. #HireSmarter

_____

_____

99

Salespeople can unknowingly sabotage their efforts with a lack of social awareness. Watch for facial expressions, tone of voice, and body language that do not match their words. This can be off-putting to buyers. #HireSmarter

_____

_____

_____

100

Hiring a salesperson is a gamble; stack the deck in your favor. —SalesFuel's Lisa Rigsby via https://aha.pub/CLeeSmith #UseData #HireSmarter

_____

_____

_____

THE ROLE OF ASSESSMENTS

Your Candidate's	Measured Pre-Hire by
Values/Beliefs	Hartman Values Profile Assessment
Motivation	Motivators Assessment
Behavior	DISC, Big 5, Myers-Briggs Assessment
Results	Sales Tendencies Assessment, Social Proof, Verifiable Sales Numbers

A DISC assessment by itself is about 80% accurate. The real value and insight comes from recognizing patterns from multiple assessments.

Share the AHA messages from this book socially by going to
https://aha.pub/HireSmarterSellMore.

Section V

The Role of Assessments in the Sales Hiring Process

Most sales managers and recruiters use assessments in the hiring process. However, some don't truly understand their role and purpose. This is why assessments are not used as effectively as they should be when hiring salespeople.

This section discusses the role of assessments in the hiring process. With the many options out there, sales managers and recruiters struggle to determine which assessments to use. What you need to realize is that one assessment only begins to tell the real story of a candidate's mindset. The patterns from multiple psychometric assessments reveal insights missed from using a personality test. A strong situational sales assessment puts it all into the context of the job you're hiring for.

Assessments can help sales managers and recruiters avoid hiring potential toxic troublemakers. They can also help you find and hire rainmakers. Just note that you cannot put all your eggs in the assessment basket. They are just one source of insight into what makes the candidate tick.

Scan the QR code or use this link to watch
the section videos:
https://aha.pub/HireSmarterSellMoreSVs

101

Using #Assessments can improve hiring outcomes. When used correctly, they can help sales managers find and hire rainmakers. #HireSmarter

_____

_____

_____

102

#Assessments enable you to measure a candidate's fit and potential objectively instead of subjectively. #HireSmarter

_____

_____

_____

103

Values/Beliefs -> Motivation -> Behavior -> Actions
-> Results. The first three are leading indicators that
#Assessments can measure. #HireSmarter

_____

_____

_____

104

Sales managers need to understand what truly drives
a candidate's actions and reactions. This is where
#Assessments can help. #HireSmarter

_____

_____

_____

105

#Assessments can help sales managers and recruiters determine if a sales candidate can exist peacefully with their coworkers, while also contributing in a meaningful way to the success of the org. #HireSmarter

---

106

Using #Assessments removes the bias that some sales managers or recruiters have unconsciously. These help sales managers and recruiters be more likely to hire a salesperson who will do well at their company. #HireSmarter

---

107

Hiring salespeople is different than filling other roles. Relying on one-size-fits-all #Assessments or personality tests from your HR department fails to put the candidate's behavior in the context of the sales job. #HireSmarter

_____

_____

_____

108

A single personality assessment won't show sales managers the complete picture of a sales candidate. They won't know a sales candidate's: 1) motivations, 2) sales skills, 3) people skills, or 4) decision-making skills. #UseData #HireSmarter

_____

_____

109

There are patterns that can emerge from looking at all assessments together in the hiring process. This allows sales managers and recruiters to spot both toxic salespeople and rainmakers. #UseData #HireSmarter

_____

_____

_____

110

#Assessments that can easily be gamed or have one right answer are of no value. Salespeople know how to game a system, so they can game a poorly constructed assessment. #HireSmarter

_____

_____

_____

111

Sales managers need to know a salesperson's motivational tendencies and what drives them. Is it power, money, fame, or learning? #Assessments #HireSmarter

_____

_____

_____

112

Sales is a results-based business. So, salespeople need to be economically motivated — not only by money, results, and competition but also by the time and energy they spend to get an ROI. #Assessments #HireSmarter

_____

_____

_____

113

When their product is complex, highly regulated, or ever-evolving, the salesperson needs to continuously learn. If the salesperson is not motivated by learning, they won't be successful selling that product. #Assessments #HireSmarter

_____

_____

_____

114

If a salesperson is too highly motivated by altruism, while their desire to help others is good, they will be too eager to discount and sacrifice profit unnecessarily. #Assessments #HireSmarter

_____

_____

_____

115

The sales profession is full of disappointments. Salespeople need to be resilient. Sales managers need to use #Assessments to determine if a few setbacks can derail a potential hire. #HireSmarter

_____

_____

_____

116

Practical thinking must be measured by your #Assessments. Today's salesperson must to be able to connect the effective use of their products/services to solving the customer's problems or achieving their goals. #HireSmarter

_____

_____

117

If they're uncoachable, they should be unhireable.
Good #Assessments indicate how open a candidate is to
coaching. Your Audition stage should put this to the test.
#HireSmarter

_____

_____

_____

118

Don't be a rebound relationship! Salespeople with
limited self-direction could be running away from the
job they were in, not running toward your job. Use
#Assessments to help determine if this is the case.
#HireSmarter

_____

_____

119

#Assessments should measure natural empathy. Emotions drive buying decisions and sales is a people business. Salespeople need to connect with customers on an emotional and logical level. #HireSmarter

120

The stress and pressure of deadlines and unrealistic goals is part of sales. #Assessments need to be able to tell you specifically how a candidate's behavior and perception by others will change under stress. #HireSmarter

121

Many successful salespeople had their career derailed by making bad decisions. Use #Assessments to measure their decision-making capabilities and hire the salesperson who can make good ones. #HireSmarter

_____

_____

_____

122

The point of a sales skills #Assessment is not to see if salespeople know how to sell. It's to understand where their strengths lie and if those match up with the core competencies required to be successful in the job. #HireSmarter

_____

_____

_____

123

#Assessments are not predictive of overall performance. They just show you what a salesperson has a tendency to do when faced with a certain situation.

_____

_____

_____

124

With printed assessments, sales managers will start from scratch every time they hire a salesperson. Using digital assessments increases efficiency. #HireSmarter
https://salesfuel.com/hire/

_____

_____

_____

125

A good assessment tool alerts hiring sales managers on what to watch for during the selection process with fast, actionable insight that doesn't require a high-priced consultant to understand. https://salesfuel.com/hire/ #HireSmarter

---

126

Good hiring assessments will give suggested interview questions based on their profile. This allows sales managers to gracefully pounce on toxic salespeople who already know standard interview questions. #HireSmarter

127

Multiple #Assessments are required to determine if a candidate has a propensity for toxicity. Recognizing these patterns is a @SalesFuel exclusive. #HireSmarter

_____

_____

_____

128

Sales managers should find a good assessment tool that goes beyond a personality or aptitude test. It should be one that can #UseData to categorize sales candidates to help determine if they're the right person. #HireSmarter

_____

_____

_____

129

#Assessments have limitations. They do not measure integrity. They do not measure psychological problems. Only a trained therapist should be relied upon to make a diagnosis of psychosis. #HireSmarter

_____

_____

_____

130

#Assessments by themselves are not a solution. The solution is using the insights they reveal (in combination with what you learn from interviews and auditions) to make smarter, less risky hiring decisions. #HireSmarter

_____

_____

_____

THE CANDIDATE'S PROFILE HELPS REVEAL THEIR FOUR FITS

You can even use the insight from the candidate's profile to give you a fair-unfair advantage when negotiating their compensation package.

Share the AHA messages from this book socially by going to
https://aha.pub/HireSmarterSellMore.

Section VI

Remember This Before You Make the Offer

There's no shortcut in hiring salespeople, much less in hiring rainmakers. You can't just rely on their track record—even if you could verify it with confidence. Past performance is not always indicative of future success.

This section shares common sense best practices to help sales teams, managers, and recruiters hire smarter and add high-potential salespeople to their team.

Scan the QR code or use this link to watch
the section videos:
https://aha.pub/HireSmarterSellMoreSVs

131

The #1 responsibility of a sales manager is to hire, coach, and develop a high-performing sales team. They need to continually strive to #HireSmarter and bring on more rainmakers.

_____

_____

_____

132

#UseData and involve others to protect yourself against making a toxic hiring mistake. You'll avoid a heavy cost mentally, emotionally, financially, and even physically. #HireSmarter

_____

_____

_____

133

A sales manager's options are not limited to Candidate A or Candidate B. They can also consider option C, none of the above. #HireSmarter

_____

_____

_____

134

Remember, the best hiring decision that a sales manager can make may be the one they don't make. #HireSmarter

_____

_____

_____

135

If you pay peanuts, you'll attract monkeys. Sales managers need to fight for the budget they need to hire (and keep) top-quality sales talent. #HireSmarter

_____

_____

_____

136

If your goal is to hire a B player, and you fall short,
you'll hire a C player. Always aspire to hire potential
rainmakers. #HireSmarter

_____

_____

_____

137

Can't find a rainmaker? The best sales candidate may
be a B player with the mindset to become an A player.
#HireSmarter

_____

_____

_____

138

Sales managers and recruiters shouldn't be too quick to dismiss salespeople who lack experience. If they have the right mindset, they can become rainmakers. #HireSmarter

_____

_____

_____

139

Your best candidate might be right under your nose. They could be working in a different role, a different department, or another location, hungry for an opportunity for advancement. #HireSmarter

_____

_____

_____

140

After leadership, sales is the most important position that a company hires for. Are you hiring the right salespeople and avoiding toxic misfits? #HireSmarter

_____

_____

_____

140+1

In the real-world story made famous in the book, *Moneyball*, and the movie of the same name, Oakland A's general manager, Billy Beane, used analytics to build a winning baseball team from scraps and gain a competitive advantage. He surprised his competitors, who clung to the old ways of making personnel decisions. These days, every franchise in professional sports uses analytics.

The number-one responsibility of a sales manager is to hire, coach, and develop a high-performing sales team. You need to continually strive to Hire Smarter and bring on more rainmakers whenever you can. The competition for this talent is fierce—and your opponents may already be using the metrics described in this book.

The best time to deploy talent analytics is early in during the hiring process, before each candidate's first interview. A comprehensive profile will help you weed out candidates who won't make the cut, before you waste time on them.

The candidate profile also gives you critical insights to help determine if they are a fit for: the job, the sales manager, your company, and the customer (the "four fits"). It should include at least three scientifically proven psychometric assessments—behavioral, motivational, and decision-making—and a top-notch sales aptitude assessment to put them all into context. Using just one assessment only gives you part of the story.

You can even use the insight from assessments to give you a fair-unfair advantage when negotiating the compensation package.

Keep in mind that hiring a salesperson poses a unique set of challenges that you won't encounter when hiring other personnel. Even the not-so-great candidates will have the gift of gab, the ability to spin facts and numbers, and they'll be very likeable. The candidate's profile acts as a second set of eyes to level the playing field. You'll quickly find the data will enhance your ability to select your next salesperson logically.

Lastly, be very mindful of toxic personalities. Use the assessments, plus what you see, hear, and feel, to avoid setting your team back with a regrettable hire. You only have to make this mistake once to know you'll never want to relive that kind of drama.

Simply stated, for your team to sell more, you have to hire smarter. How good are you at using talent analytics to make the best hiring decisions possible?

Appendix

The 13 Toxic Types of Salespeople

According to Webster, toxicity means "containing or being poisonous material especially when capable of causing death or serious debilitation; exhibiting symptoms of infection or toxicosis; extremely harsh, malicious, or harmful . . ."

A toxic salesperson makes others worse—lowering their performance by draining time, energy, and positivity that should be used for increasing revenue.

—C. Lee Smith

At one time or another, every sales manager feels like they are stepping into an abyss. They have to replace the sales rep who just left, or they're tasked with expanding their department to meet the challenge of growing sales for the company. Either way, they have to make a big decision.

The candidate sitting in front of them could be an outstanding addition to the team—or they could be the manager's worst nightmare. Hiring an employee who turns out to be toxic can cost the company lost sales, higher rates of sales rep turnover, and turmoil. Research shows that 1 percent of people are psychopaths and 4 percent are sociopaths, while another 2-3 percent of the population might end up behaving in a toxic way in the workplace. When you add it up, that's nearly one out of twelve people.

Those numbers might not sound high, but in a small company, where one employee in ten is toxic, you're dealing with 10 percent of the workforce. Soon, you're rushing around putting out fires caused by the unhealthy behavior exhibited by one or more of your employees. At the very least, work may not be getting done. Worst-case outcomes range from multiple key staff members leaving the company to expensive payoffs to rid yourself of your toxic employee.

You can avoid these situations by understanding how toxicity develops in a workplace. Steve Sisler, of Behavioral Resources Group, says that three conditions in the workplace are conducive to toxic behavior. An employee:

- Might not like or be capable of the work they are asked to do
- May have trouble interacting with the other members of their team
- May have trouble interacting with their supervisor

What immediately comes to mind for most managers is the desire to keep employees with toxic tendencies out of their organizations. They hope to do this during the hiring process.

On the surface, a candidate may look outstanding. But in the real world, human behavior is complex. Managers should remember that all employees come to work with two agendas. They know what they want from the workplace, their co-workers, and the higher-ups. They also have to deal with what other employees want from them.

In your workplace, your current mix of employees and managers may balance each other well, all fitting into the corporate culture. When it's time to hire a new employee, balancing the behavioral tendencies of a candidate against the skill set you need and the environment of the hiring department is a judgment call.

People with a strong power- or attention-getting orientation may be exactly what you need to shake things up. In a different setting, however, these folks can wreak havoc on a corporate culture. Managers usually pick up on employees with a strong power orientation quickly. Other new hires may exhibit toxic behavior that's harder to detect but can be just as damaging to an organization.

Managers should also know that new hires aren't the only ones who conduct themselves in a toxic manner. An employee who gets transferred into a new position or department can suddenly begin behaving in a way that team members haven't seen before. The cool, calm, and collected benefits manager suddenly turns secretive and hoards information when they take over payroll processing. The efficient webmaster starts reminding everyone of the rules and won't give out passwords to security offenders.

Is there any way for managers avoid these situations? Absolutely. Formal psychometric assessments can reduce the margin of error in hiring and promotions . A good assessment system won't necessarily tell you if a person is going to act up in your organization. But if that person is going to cause problems, a good assessment system will tell you the type of behavior they'll have a propensity to exhibit.

Dr. William Marston once described four basic behavioral traits in a system we call DISC: dominant, influence, steadiness, and compliant. These traits are associated with specific strengths, weaknesses, fears, and motivators. Most candidate assessment systems based on DISC will indicate how an applicant will fare in a specific job environment. These systems fall short of identifying the type of toxic behavior that a candidate might display once they are on the job.

In this book, we offer a glimpse at thirteen types of toxic personality types we've identified in the workplace for sales teams. We have ordered them from the most difficult and problematic, the Jungle Fighter, to the least likely to be problematic, the Martyr. Using documented case studies, we also outline the steps you can take to address toxic behavior and restore harmony to your organization. In some cases, you may be able to adjust the work environment and coach employees who exhibit toxic behavior. In other cases, the best strategy may be to avoid hiring employees with toxic behavioral tendencies in the first place. If they are already on the payroll, though, you'll have no choice but to get them out of your organization.

Toxic Type #1 — The Jungle Fighter

Common behaviors exhibited by Jungle Fighters include:

- Being blunt, cutting, overly aggressive, and impatient
- Seeing people as tools only for their usefulness
- Attacking coworkers (and their work) with a kill-or-be-killed mindset.
- Trampling others to gain control and subject people to warlike conditions in hopes that coworkers will surrender to their will and unreasonable demands.

If you're dealing with a Jungle Fighter, brace yourself. You're in for a difficult test of your management skills. You'll never encounter a behavior that is more toxic or problematic to your company culture.

I had hired plenty of people before I encountered a Jungle Fighter. This time, however, our screening process failed. The Jungle Fighter interviewed well and came across as a strong candidate during testing. We quickly hired this person whom we hoped would accomplish great things with us. During the first few weeks of employment at my company, the Jungle Fighter settled in. At my suggestion, this individual took key employees to lunch to form stronger bonds and to learn the details of our business.

Before long, the Jungle Fighter began coming into my office to warn me. Did I realize that a specific long-term employee was underperforming? Soon after, the Jungle Fighter suggested that one of our top performers wasn't a very big asset to the company.

I began to question myself. Had I missed these key details about existing employees? Maybe I'd gone on autopilot and overlooked big problems that were only obvious to a new employee.

I started to pay closer attention. That's when a couple of employees hinted that the new hire I was so excited about, the Jungle Fighter, was a potential problem. I didn't want to believe it at first. Then, I heard through informal channels that the Jungle Fighter was pretty sure that they could outclass me as CEO.

As a small business owner, it didn't take long to make my decision. The Jungle Fighter had to go. Luckily, the buck stops with me at my company.

But the experience got me thinking. In a larger organization, Jungle Fighters can wreak havoc. If they have the upper brass fooled into thinking that they're great contributors and they are actually performing well, they'll be left alone. They'll cut a path of destruction through one department after another as they battle their way to the top.

Employees will be gossiping about why you can't see the truth. Even worse, they'll start looking around for other positions.

Once a Jungle Fighter has infiltrated your workplace, it's not easy to oust them. They will turn that kill-or-be-killed mindset on you when they realize a termination is in the works. Don't be afraid to call in reinforcements. In a large organization, get the HR department involved. In a smaller company, bite the financial bullet and hire an employment attorney who can provide the expert advice you need.

The most nerve-wracking aspect of dealing with these individuals is that they don't always infiltrate organizations. They could be in your company, undetected, until a manager unwittingly promotes them. That's what happened to the owner of an electrical company who put a competent project manager in charge of a department. The owner figured the project manager would be as good at managing people as he was at managing workflow.

The owner didn't realize that when the newly promoted department head took on the task of managing people, he turned "mean as sin." Before long, people began leaving the company. The guy was so controlling that no employee wanted to put up with him. By the time the owner figured out what was going on, only one employee remained in the department.

This project manager's angry demeanor started to worry the owner. If he let the guy go, was he going to have problems with him? Was retaliation a possibility? Likely so.

The owner called in an outside consultant. After reviewing the situation, the consultant suggested the employee be signed up for mandatory coaching. Everyone hoped the outcome would be a peaceful resignation.

During the first coaching session, the Jungle Fighter sat far back in his chair. He crossed his arms. Before the coach had a chance to speak, the Jungle Fighter barked out, "What do you want to talk about?"

His approach to coaching was just as unreasonable as his method of supervising people. In his supervisory role, he sensed passive management in the organization. That situation gave him the opening to do what he wanted. The coach understood the organizational dynamics and developed a plan. He outlined, in great detail, what the coaching program would involve. When the Jungle Fighter heard what the coaching plan involved, he realized the atmosphere at work had changed. He would now be held accountable for his behavior. Even worse, he was dealing with a neutral third party, not the passive managers who had been overlooking the way he trampled his team members.

The Jungle Fighter never showed up for a second coaching session and left the company soon after. The owner was relieved to have avoided a nasty confrontation or perhaps even a lawsuit. But he still lost plenty. Imagine the expense involved as the company began recruiting for replacement employees. During the Jungle Fighter's reign of toxicity, the company missed the opportunity to win new business. They likely took a few knocks to their reputation that took a while to improve.

These negative outcomes could have been avoided if the owner had asked the Jungle Fighter to take a battery of behavioral assessments before he promoted him.

Toxic Type #2 — The Exploiter

Common behaviors exhibited by Exploiters include:

- Being hostile, independent, quick, and arbitrary
- Becoming a danger to others as they resist established rules, policies, and protocols
- Distorting information for personal gain and gambling more than they can afford to pay
- Failing to recognize dangerous situations, refusing to course-correct, and remaining excessively stubborn
- Showing zero tolerance for rules and fearing loss of control

Like the Jungle Fighter, the Exploiter fears losing control. They have a strong desire to enhance their position in the organization and with clients. On the scale of toxic behavior, they're likely to create problems with their manager and their coworkers.

In one professional organization, the Exploiter, who was also the boss, wasn't keeping track of what was happening with an important client. Maybe she felt she didn't need to because she believed in making her own rules.

During an important conference call, the Exploiter promised a client she could get them the coverage they sought in a prestigious national newspaper. The staff members, listening in on the call, had to bite their tongues. They'd already tried and failed to get the client coverage in that publication. The Exploiter's behavior was a clear violation of industry protocol: never promise what you can't deliver.

After the call, the boss checked in with her staff and asked where they stood with that big publication. When they explained the situation, she was outraged. She'd made a promise and she wouldn't back down. She had a reputation to maintain. Her staff had to find a way to carry out the promise she'd made—or else.

Her team members were outraged too. But what recourse did they have? They had no choice but to follow her orders or find another job.

The Exploiter failed to see how her toxic behavior was demoralizing her staff. She likely told herself that good help was hard to find while she replaced employees who kept leaving. Exploiters, in DISC terminology, are often dominant individuals and the least likely to identify themselves as the root of the problem. They typically refuse to try to change their behavior. As a coworker, an Exploiter can cut a mean path through an organization. Exploiters will dig for information they can use to their own personal advantage. When the information doesn't match what they want to hear, they'll distort it. The Exploiter will also use information against a coworker to get what they want—whether it's a better assignment or ultimate control over team members.

Once coworkers become aware of the Exploiter's true motivations, they'll stop sharing information. They'll leave them out of email communications. Before a manager realizes it, the team has ceased to function effectively. Misinformation is rampant because nobody trusts the Exploiter. Depending on how rigid the Exploiter is, the manager may have no choice but to show them the door.

Toxic Type #3 — The Taskmaster

Common behaviors exhibited by Taskmasters include:

- Forcing commitments
- Impeding others through impatience
- Demanding unreasonable efforts from others
- Giving the silent treatment to those who cramp their style
- Becoming punitive and subjecting other people's ideas to rigorous examination through interrogation and intimidation

The Taskmaster often seems like a manager's dream employee. Here is an individual who will get things done. In fact, they are often so good at completing projects, they work their way into management roles. At that point, their behavior can quickly turn toxic and problematic. Taskmasters can be as problematic as Exploiters in an organization.

One Taskmaster, the manager of a movie theater, was all smiles and promises when he hired a young worker. He promised to accommodate the worker's other commitments with flexible scheduling. In his quest to keep the theater operating smoothly, this Taskmaster forgot his promise. He booked the employee for a shift when she had an unavoidable conflict. The employee quickly contacted him about the conflict and explained that she'd been unable to find anyone to fill in for her. The Taskmaster's response was, "Find someone to cover your shift or forfeit your post." The manager displayed no empathy. He likely justified his attitude by rationalizing that he was taking care of business. In this case, the employee quit.

As a manager, a Taskmaster can exhibit other kinds of toxic behavior. They'll set high standards for work quality, but they won't take the time to explain how the work should be done. Without coaching, employees flounder and the Taskmaster simply grows more impatient. Taskmasters can also demand extraordinary work effort from team members and then fail to thank them.

On the road to completing work, the Taskmaster as a coworker can leave carnage. If a coworker questions them or asks for five extra minutes to proofread their report, the Taskmaster retaliates—often by ignoring them during the next meeting. If that coworker later comes up with a good idea, the Taskmaster will squelch it. To make matters worse, Taskmasters understand they possess superior skills, and they often expect compliments for projects they've completed. After a while, the entire team's performance starts to suffer. Sooner or later, in the case of an extreme Taskmaster, everyone will have felt bullied by this individual.

Managers often don't see the Taskmaster's behavior from a coworker perspective. They fail to understand the negative impact on the organization. They only see that the work is getting done. Even better, the manager reasons, they don't have to worry because the Taskmaster is keeping everyone on track.

One of the only ways for coworkers to succeed in their quest to change the Taskmaster's approach is to form a group to talk with the manager. If the manager is too enthralled with the Taskmaster's success, they may not take any action. In the long term, the manager will only understand the situation after they have to replace good people who leave the organization because of the abuse taken from the Taskmaster. At that point, after culture and productivity suffers, the Taskmaster may also be terminated.

That's what happened at an architectural firm in the Midwest. For over a decade, an architect with outstanding design skills had one key goal. He wanted to be a manager and he kept asking for the promotion. The business owner had reservations, and he asked the architect to take an assessment. The results confirmed what the owner already suspected: The brilliant architect was not a people person.

The guy's empathy scores turned out to be extremely low. He remained emotionally distant from the other staff members and seemed unable to change. In a management role, he likely would have demanded unreasonable excellence from members of his department and would have demoralized them. The owner eventually had to let his architect go because the guy insisted on being a manager and refused to stay in his current role.

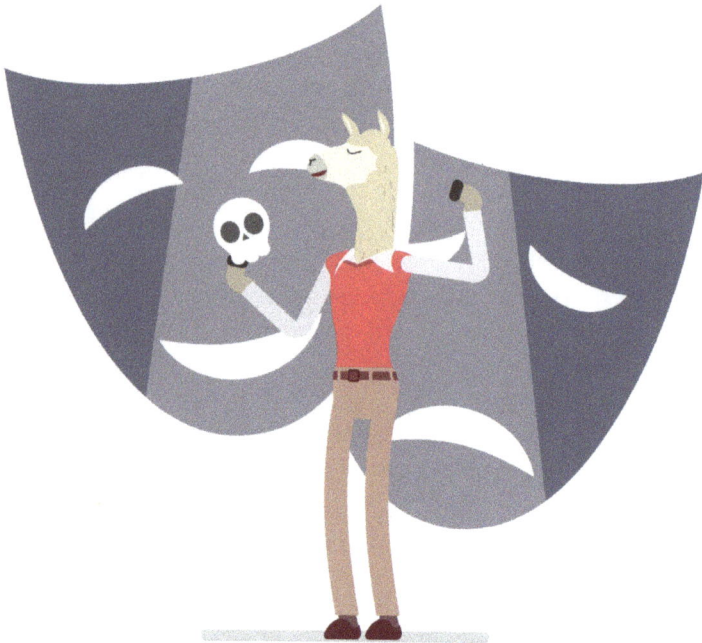

Toxic Type #4 — The Drama Llama

Common behaviors exhibited by Drama Llamas include:

- Striving to be the center of attention
- Being emotionally needy
- Looking busy but not producing anything

People who've worked with a Drama Llama will tell you that they are exhausted at the end of the day. Tears, door slamming, and people running out of the room are common experiences when a Drama Llama is part of the team. At first, they'll come across as truly caring friends. They'll insist they are trying to help. That's because the Drama Llama insists on playing a role in various situations. Before long, they make most situations all about them.

As seen through the lens of the DISC theory of human behavior, Drama Llamas rank as high influencers. A typical influencer possesses energy, loves generating high-level ideas, and enjoys engaging with people. Drama Llamas are influencers at an extreme level. They feed on emotion, exhibit spontaneity, and do not focus on details or methodical tasks.

At their core, Drama Llamas are emotionally needy. They fear not being liked, and that fear causes them to get too involved with the needs of coworkers. Some members of the team may not appreciate this overreach. They may prefer to solve their problems on their own. When they rebuff the Drama Llama's attempts at "helping," watch out. The Drama Llama will react negatively. They'll make inappropriate comments or even physically push the perceived offender.

The Drama Llama reacts this way because they fear failing. If they are not part of the company's in-group, they'll also lash out. Their negative behavior reveals their poor self-esteem. They may complain that they're being taken advantage of. In truth, they need to perceive that they've been taken advantage of, so they can create drama. They undervalue their good qualities, as well as their weaker qualities, which means they won't work on improving themselves.

The constant turmoil surrounding a Drama Llama wears out coworkers. They'll try to avoid this individual, because the frequent interactions can negatively impact their productivity.

Managing a Drama Llama can also be challenging. At one company, the Drama Llama had convinced the boss to hire a specific vendor for an event. The Drama Llama had a personal relationship with this vendor. During the event, the Drama Llama planned to let everyone know how important their role was in connecting the company to this vendor. However, when time ran short, the boss decided to cut out the Drama Llama's presentation. The Drama Llama accused the boss of not being supportive and ran out of the meeting, crying. The other team members were left wondering what had happened. Their concern for the Drama Llama's wellbeing shifted the focus away from the important event. The boss was left to deal with the uncomfortable situation.

Team members who supervise Drama Llamas must recognize what they're dealing with quickly. Instead of allowing these individuals to push their buttons, they should remain calm and remove emotion from the situation. If the Drama Llama claims that another employee is incompetent and that they could do a better job, managers should ask for specifics. What part of the job is the other employee failing at and what exactly would the Drama Llama do to improve productivity? At that point, the Drama Llama will likely fall apart because they are not detail-oriented individuals. Managers may be able to help Drama Llamas stay on track by insisting on emotion-free meetings. In some cases, managers may have to terminate the Drama Llama in order to repair the company culture these individuals often destroy.

Toxic Type #5 — The Instigator

Common behaviors exhibited by Instigators include:

- Resisting without a known cause
- Demoralizing others, cutting others short, and finishing their sentences
- Being hyper-inflexible
- Patronizing and imposing personal values on others
- Resisting pleasing others and never stating their "real" position
- Ignoring weaker people-types and expecting them to know what to do
- Having an opinionated approach that keeps people in line

Organizational Instigators possess strong personalities. They also have plenty of energy. When the manager doesn't keep the Instigator busy with challenging tasks, they can expect difficulties to arise in the organization. That's because the Instigator will belittle other employees. They'll put down the ideas of others and come off as judgmental and condescending.

With a bit of the Jungle Fighter in them, Instigators are not always focused on the same goals as the team. In fact, they don't really want to be on the team. They just want the satisfaction of always being right. In a team setting, an Instigator will give you as much trouble as a Taskmaster.

With their direct and blunt approach, Instigators quickly put off others in the organization. Coworkers look for ways to avoid them. They know that if they go to the Instigator for help on a project, they're likely to get a lecture instead of assistance. Company resources get drained while employees try to figure out how to leave Instigators out of meetings.

With their tendency to impose their personal values on others, Instigators can make other employees feel uncomfortable. In one case, an Instigator always made it a point to tell a coworker to smile more. Whether they were in the break room, the conference room, or a cubicle, the message was always the same. This imposition of his personal value on the coworker created an uncomfortable work environment. The "unsmiling" employee soon learned to avoid the Instigator.

When an Instigator lands a management position, employees have reason to worry. Instigators will play favorites. They'll team up with a person who shares their values. Other employees are left to fend for themselves, and since they're avoiding the Instigator, leadership can expect a hit to the bottom line.

Fortunately, Instigators are one of the rarest of the toxic personality types.

Toxic Type #6 — The Vacillator

Common behaviors exhibited by Vacillators include:

- Getting offensive when challenged and egotistical when flattered
- Creating emotional tension regarding expectations
- Remaining indecisive until the situation is critical
- Using excessive logic without emotions and imposing excessive standards of perfection on those who are less careful

This toxic behavior may be stoked by the environment the employee is entering. Organizations that need a thoughtful deliberative employee who works well alone might find a Vacillator to be the perfect hire. But if you're seeking an employee to join your fast-paced environment, be on the lookout for toxic Vacillator tendencies.

Vacillators get nothing done. They want to slow the work process down. They can't make up their minds because they fear they will be wrong. Their anxiety and insecurity means they'll stall for time. They will avoid team members who they perceive as taking big risks. In this context, they can be as problematic to the team environment as Taskmasters and Instigators.

While you're waiting for their answer on whether you should invest in a partnership, your Vacillator is off running permutations of various outcomes. They'll tell you they need more information before they can give you a thumbs-up. If you push them to move quickly, they'll inform you that you're not being careful enough in making this big decision. Paralysis by analysis is a common occurrence for the Vacillator.

One Vacillator made a great impression on a CEO who insisted he wanted this individual to join the company as a high-level manager on his leadership team. The new employee possessed many fine credentials. During the hiring process, he also negotiated a sweet separation deal.

Before long, the rest of the C-suite members realized the new hire was operating on a separate track from them. They always contributed their deliverables to projects on time. The new hire simply did not work at their speed. He'd consistently ask for more time before making key decisions. The company's progress in a competitive marketplace was held up while he worried and stressed and did everything except come to a decision.

In the end, the rest of the executive team reached their own decision. They realized they'd made an expensive mistake. They'd hired an individual whose behavior didn't match the way the rest of the team worked. The company paid a substantial sum to send the Vacillator on his way.

Toxic Type #7 — The Glory Hog

Common behaviors exhibited by Glory Hogs include:

- Having a high need for approval
- Taking credit and recognition at every opportunity—even when it is not deserved
- Being verbally aggressive

On motivational assessments, Glory Hogs score so high for Individuality that it becomes a need, not just something they desire. Their insatiable need for recognition drives them to seek out situations where they can be noticed making the big sale or saving that important account.

As a team member, they will take credit for successes and won't acknowledge anyone else's part in the win. On a basketball team, for example, a Glory Hog would be called a "Ball Hog."

But when a project doesn't go well, as in the team losing the sale, the Glory Hog will deflect taking any responsibility. They'll look for a way to blame everyone else. This behavior contrasts with what a conscientious manager would do: accept the blame and share the credit.

In the workplace, the need to have constant approval and take credit when credit isn't due quickly becomes toxic. Coworkers begin to distrust the Glory Hog and the behavior ultimately stifles cooperation.

Another behavior that team members find off-putting is the Glory Hog's tendency to dominate the conversation. This happens whether they are talking with just one other person or in groups. Steve Sisler reports that "their nervous energy causes them to not stop talking."

Glory Hogs share the fear of not being liked with another toxic type, The Drama Llama. Glory Hogs need validation in recognition from others to prove themselves wrong. However, Drama Llamas need to be wronged or underappreciated to prove themselves right.

Obsession with recognition can get Glory Hogs into big trouble. A sportscaster who was a little carried away with his image learned an important lesson the hard way. A Glory Hog, the sportscaster completely lost his cool after a set of technical glitches caused him to look awkward, multiple times, in front of his adoring TV fans. In that situation, some people would have taken a few laps around the track until they cooled off. In this case, the individual grew increasingly paranoid that the station manager was making him look bad on purpose. One day, after another technical glitch, the Glory Hog exploded. He grabbed the guy that he thought was dissing him—the station manager—and pinned him against the desk.

The station manager suffered no serious injury, but he knew he had a problem. The Glory Hog's toxic behavior threatened employee safety. He had no empathy for the fact that the station manager was having equipment trouble. All along, the manager, as part of a team effort, was trying to make the Glory Hog look his best. After the event, the Glory Hog apologized, but it was too little, too late. While he was wildly popular with viewers, the station manager couldn't take the chance that this individual's toxic behavior would surface again. The Glory Hog's behavior resulted in those two dreaded words: "You're fired."

Toxic Type #8 — The Job Protector

Common behaviors exhibited by Job Protectors include:

- Pushing back at any change to their day-to-day routine
- Addressing new directives with an abundance of caution and guarding their role on the team and in the company
- Eventually coming around but often resisting at first

Job Protectors don't have issues working with other people. But they're terrified of change in their work process. On the scale of toxic behaviors, Job Protectors are only situationally problematic.

When managers introduce a new tool, the Job Protector will find a reason not to use it. You may be showing off the latest mobile phone and telling everyone how the device will save them time and aggravation at work. The techies in your department will latch onto the device, figure out exactly how it works, and find cool new features that you missed. The Job Protector will be cringing. They'll be gripping the desk in panic mode, believing that the device will change everything about the way they work. Even worse, that efficient new device may threaten their paychecks.

Job Protectors are typically low-energy employees. They are comfortable in their existing routines. Often, they're older workers who also seem befuddled by the latest technology.

This attitude may be slightly amusing at first. You may not mind helping them learn how to upgrade their skills. Younger team members might also be willing to lend them a hand. But over time, Job Protectors create a toxic work environment.

They slow down progress. Eventually, coworkers may begin to avoid Job Protectors or work around them. That behavior is a signal that managers must pick up on. Don't allow Job Protectors to disturb coworkers because they can't figure out how to do their own jobs. Managers should ask the Job Protector to take a class to upgrade their skills. If your Job Protector won't agree to improve themselves, you have a choice. You can either ask them to leave the organization, or you can accept that you are running a charity and aren't maximizing profits.

Toxic Type #9 — The Agitator

Common behaviors exhibited by Agitators include:

- Keeping an emotional distance from others and guarding their time from those who waste it
- Creating an impenetrable wall between themselves and others
- Becoming easily agitated while agitating their coworkers
- Preferring objects to people, acting evasively, fearing vulnerability, and becoming too matter-of-fact

Agitators often have great skills and capabilities. As a solo contributor, an Agitator can make a big difference on the bottom line for an organization. But they don't enjoy collaborating and may even show suspicion toward coworkers. The last thing they want is to spend time helping a coworker.

In a management role, Agitators can quickly exhibit toxic behavior. These managers come into the office and close their door at 8:30 a.m. They don't do management by walking around (MBWA). They also don't say good morning or spend time with team members, finding out how they are doing. Agitators typically score as high C's and D's on the DISC system. Remember that high C's are detail oriented. Team members with high D tendencies are driven to get the job done. With this profile, impatient Agitators don't want to be slowed down. A good assessment system will reveal Agitator potential and help you keep these individuals out of management roles in your organization.

Managers like Agitators because they get the job done. Over time, these individuals can gain substantial control over an organization's assets. During this process, they won't call attention to themselves. But they do appreciate the prestige and recognition that comes when they successfully accomplish difficult tasks. Agitators can also have hoarder tendencies, especially when it comes to information. In that capacity, they can also be dangerous to an organization's success.

The Agitator's behavior becomes toxic when they won't interact or share their power base with others. Coworkers will be well aware of Agitators in an organization. They can be as toxic as Exploiters and Taskmasters to an organization's cultures. Your other employees will also be looking for reasons to avoid them.

One of the worst managerial fears in today's digital economy is network vulnerability. What will happen if we get hacked and are faced with the need to pay a ransom to gain access to our data? This is a question that business leaders ask regularly, and all too frequently, they are asking the question after they receive a ransom demand.

In one company, the managers grew concerned that one of their own employees would make a ransom demand regarding network access. The Agitator had gained plenty of organizational power over time. He was extremely competent and managed to get himself into the position where he was the sole person in charge of system passwords. He loved having control over valuable assets. The company's leaders didn't share his enthusiasm. What would they do if he quit? What if there was a serious health crisis and they couldn't communicate with the employee? What if the guy grew disgruntled some day? They'd never get the passwords.

Senior management looked for a way out of the situation and finally hired a coach who had a series of conversations to help the Agitator relax his way of thinking and share the passwords.

Not every Agitator situation will work out so well. The longer the Agitator exerts control, the more expensive and difficult they can become to resolve. Managers should stay alert to anyone in the organization who could be building a power base. They should insist on power sharing and on cross-training to cut down on vulnerability.

Toxic Type #10 — The Cynic

Common behaviors exhibited by Cynics include:

- Trusting no one and taking nothing at face value
- Assuming others will take advantage of them and shutting people out with no explanation
- Letting coworkers survive on their own and operating alone, even when in groups
- Becoming jerk-like (to put it politely) when others oppose their views and considering a select few for interrogation-like understanding
- Demanding inappropriate compensation for work tasks

Cynics are suspicious by nature. Dating back to the age of Greek philosophers, they believe that humans let selfishness drive their actions. When something new and different comes along, Cynics will find a reason to reject it. They'll suspect that person pitching the idea is incompetent or up to no good. They have low trust in their coworkers and in management.

The toxic part of a Cynic's behavior stems from their tendency to make negative comments about coworkers and managers they don't trust. Like Instigators, Cynics want to form relationships with peers who feel the way they do. Once they team up and influence others, the poison they spread in an organization creates a significant management challenge.

Cynics often feel like they are being taken advantage of economically. They'll complain that they are not being paid enough. To reinforce their negative position, some Cynics will dig in their heels and refuse to accept what a manager is asking them to do. They'll debate with the manager about why the new idea is no good. They're often pessimistic about the future.

Over time, some managers may be able to coach Cynics to be consciously aware of their actions. This awareness can help them think clearly about other ways to respond when a change is introduced. Some Cynics won't budge. With their mindset of negativity firmly entrenched, the manager may have to show them the door.

Toxic Type #11 — The Lone Wolf

Common behaviors exhibited by Lone Wolves (not to be confused with the seller profile of the same name in The Challenger Sale) include:

- Keeping an emotional distance from others, demanding privacy, refusing vulnerability, and rarely communicating personal ideas
- Taking things too seriously when reacting to unexpected events
- Acting punitively toward themselves, holding themselves to impossible standards, and becoming overly intense when failing to realize goals

Have you ever worked with someone whose actions make the hair on the back of your neck stand up? If the answer is yes, then you may have encountered a Lone Wolf. This individual makes everyone feel a little uneasy. They're obsessed with personal privacy and usually emotionally distant. In an organizational setting, their behavior is likely to be problematic.

While the rest of us might spend a few minutes in the break room sharing what we did over the weekend, the Lone Wolf will be in their cubicle doing something else in secrecy. That tendency makes us uneasy. First, they make us feel slightly guilty because we know we should be working too. But more importantly, we don't know anything about the Lone Wolf. We spend a third of our lives with our co-workers. We want to get to know them, to understand what's happening in their lives. The truth is, we know nothing about the Lone Wolf in our midst.

Many coworkers believe the Lone Wolf won't get emotional. In fact, the opposite is true. The Lone Wolf can get emotional about their own job performance. When they don't succeed at a difficult task, they can act punitive to themselves.

Managers might try to console a Lone Wolf who's struggling, but they'll often be rebuffed. Why? The Lone Wolf doesn't want to show vulnerability. Despite being put off, managers should continue to encourage an employee who exhibits Lone Wolf behavior and not let them spiral down.

While a Lone Wolf can exist at any level in an organization, they're often drawn to starting and running their own businesses. In the role of entrepreneur, the Lone Wolf's tendency toward excellence can help the organization grow. Over time, however, these same traits can stop a business from thriving. Lone Wolves must learn to let go of certain tasks and focus on more strategic work. Most Lone Wolves can't accomplish this transition. They continue to believe that only they can make decisions. To stay in control, they'll keep information to themselves. Their direct reports won't know what is going on, and that's the kind of behavior that is toxic to a company.

Take the case of the Lone Wolf who managed to grow his organization to a good size over a couple of decades. He was ready to retire. As part of the vetting process, prospective buyers were talking to employees about what it was like to work in the organization.

The employees showed no positivity about the future of the business, and that attitude scared off the prospects. The problem was that employees could never get a read on the owner. They weren't sure where he stood on anything. In that work environment, employees don't feel engaged or committed.

The owner realized that he had a problem. He reached out to get help on how to open up and communicate with others. Not every Lone Wolf will work hard on self-improvement.

In another case, the board of directors hired a turnaround CEO who exhibited Lone Wolf behavior from the first day of employment. During work hours, he was inaccessible. He kept his door closed. Nobody could get past his personal assistant who screened all visitors, calls, and emails.

When a manager had an idea about making a change, they had to submit it in writing to the Lone Wolf. He read the email and then emailed back his response. This process sometimes took him three days—no discussion, no team meeting. His direct reports started to think the guy had ice water running through his veins. Before long, the managers who thought they'd participate in the turnaround grew frustrated. They'd been promised retention bonuses, but they had no idea how things were going or if their input was meaningful. Several of those employees left before the turnaround of the company was completed.

Toxic Type #12 — The Enforcer

Common behaviors exhibited by Enforcers include:

- Having strict thought streams, believing things must be done a certain way, and creating an emotional distance from others
- Never telling you where they stand on the issues but becoming punitive when rules are broken
- Holding a grudge and possibly becoming vindictive when crossed

Anyone who has watched hockey over the years knows that many teams have an Enforcer. If a player on the opposite team causes an injury, watch out. The Enforcer will even the score. They'll often do this knowing full well that they'll spend time in the penalty box. Why? Because the "end justifies the means." The Enforcer will behave the same way in your company too. While not as problematic as Jungle Fighters or Taskmasters, Enforcers can cause plenty of trouble.

Enforcers insist that rules must be followed—or else. Some organizations need Enforcers. Police officers know that when a person exceeds the speed limit, they must write a ticket. In this setting, the motivators of power and rightness serve the greater good. We are all safer when Enforcers make sure citizens follow the rules. Similarly, on the battlefield, the troop leader doesn't question the orders they are given. They insist the mission will be carried out exactly as planned and practiced. Enforcers can be highly effective in situations where security and safety are necessary—think nuclear power plants.

In some organizations, Enforcers play a critical role. They often become managers because the higher-ups believe these employees will make sure the job gets done properly.

So, where does toxicity come in? It's all about this person's tendencies in the workplace environment and how well they mesh with coworkers. Like Jungle Fighters and Instigators, Enforcers do not easily mix with other people.

If a manager puts an Enforcer in charge of a creative effort, trouble will follow. Instead of encouraging their team members to think creatively about an ad campaign, the Enforcer will worry about the rules. If there's a paper clip shortage in the company, they'll worry about how many paper clips an employee used during a meeting. They absolutely will not approve of employees riding scooters down the hallways in order to tap into creativity. They'll point out that doing so is prohibited in the employee manual.

An Enforcer's behavior can quickly become toxic if an employee has dared to complain about them. They don't accept negative feedback as an opportunity to self-reflect and improve. Instead of thinking about how to change their behavior to become a better team player, they'll look for an opportunity for payback.

With an Enforcer on the staff, team members might be looking over their shoulders as they walk out to the company parking lot at night. With that kind of stress brewing in an organization, you'll see employee turnover before long.

Toxic Type #13 — The Martyr

Common behaviors exhibited by Martyrs include:

- Having low energy, avoiding conflict, and only complaining to safe people who will sympathize with their feelings
- Pouting or moping when they feel sidelined or overlooked
- Never revealing where they actually stand on the issues
- Telling you that everything is fine, but everything is most certainly not fine

The Martyr can be one of the most charming individuals in an organization. They're often well-liked by their peers. On the toxic behavior scale, Martyrs are the least likely to make trouble in the team environment.

But they can be poison to the success of an organization because they aren't actually getting anything done. As emotional individuals, Martyrs won't say where they stand. They pout and whine. They certainly won't ask for help. In the meantime, their incompetence can wreak havoc on the bottom line.

Martyrs mask what they're unable to do. They're personable and can talk their way into a company. "Fake it until you make it" is the Martyr's motto.

Take the case of the likeable guy who interviewed well for the comptroller position in a large organization. In that role, he should have been managing investments on a daily basis to optimize interest earnings. He should have been paying bills early to take advantage of vendor discounts.

After a while, senior managers noticed that the cash flow wasn't what it should have been. But they couldn't figure out why. After talking to several employees, an outside behavioral consultant found the source of the problem. The Martyr didn't know how to do his job. Soon after that, the leadership team hired a CFO. Within eight weeks, they were generating the kind of cash flow they expected. The likeable, talkative comptroller was fired.

In another instance, a company had hired a strong candidate to develop their website. She arrived on the job with great recommendations. She also had a warm and engaging personality. For an entire year, she walked the halls with her binder, discussing the possibilities of the website she envisioned. But no actual work happened on the website. Meanwhile, the company was falling behind on achieving its goals.

Finally, on the advice of an outside expert, the employee was transferred to a new position—not surprisingly, in the public relations field. There, she found her true calling. The company went on to hire a website expert who delivered what they needed. This time, the hiring managers weren't dazzled by personality or recommendations but instead, used the results of formal assessments to find a candidate who possessed the skills and the set of behavioral tendencies needed to succeed in the position.

Because over 60 percent of resumes contain information that is not true, hiring managers must be on alert. If managers want to be certain that a candidate possesses a critical skill, they should ask for evidence. Better yet, they should have the individual produce original work showing their competence. A good candidate will turn around the request quickly. A candidate who has Martyr tendencies won't even try to complete the assignment because they won't know how.

Toxic Stew

Jungle Fighters aren't always bad people. Their toxic behavior comes from their fear of losing control. They may have been raised in an unstable environment, one that caused them to crave control over what happens in their lives. Once they get out on their own, they'll continue to exhibit the toxic behavior they learned in their youth. In the workplace, higher dominance individuals like Jungle Fighters tend to see people as tools, as a means to an end. They don't recognize that their employees have contributed to their success. Their lack of gratitude leaves people feeling used.

What happens when you mix a Martyr with a Jungle Fighter in the same organization? Everyone loses. That's what happened when two brothers started running a contracting business left to them by their father. The Martyr brother was a passive individual who didn't want confrontation. Compared to his Jungle Fighter brother, he exhibited low dominance in his behavior. The Jungle Fighter made the decisions in the business and took credit for the successes.

The Martyr had ambitions and felt plenty used. He wanted to succeed but couldn't take power in the company, not when his Jungle Fighter brother was hacking his way around. The Martyr, with his ability to talk and deceive, started working behind the scenes. He diverted money from the contracting business. He made up seven fake employees for projects he was supposedly running. Over time, he stole over $1 million to pay these "employees." He used the money to build a successful side business: a restaurant. When the scam was uncovered, a professional counselor was called in. The brothers agreed they wanted to resolve their differences. With plenty of hard work and acknowledgement of their shortcomings, the brothers continue to work together.

Not every toxic stew story ends so happily.

About the Author

C. Lee Smith helps sales teams leverage critical insights that enable them to acquire, develop and retain their best employees and customers.

He is the CEO of SalesFuel®, a sales intelligence firm he founded in 1989 that has been recognized as one of the Top 10 Sales Enablement providers worldwide by *Selling Power* magazine.

Lee is one of select few certified advisors worldwide for sales consultant Jeffrey Gitomer and was personally recognized as one of the Leading Sales Consultants by *Selling Power* magazine.

In addition to being an author and popular keynote speaker, he is also a C-Suite Network Advisor for sales leadership and co-host of the popular *Manage Smarter*™ podcast.

Lee is the creator of the SalesFuel COACH and SalesFuel HIRE SaaS platforms for hiring and coaching your best sales talent. He is also the creator of AdMall®, the leading sales intelligence platform for local media sales and digital marketing professionals.

He is also a certified Behavioral Analyst with expertise in the destructive impact toxic employees have on your sales team.

Lee is a graduate of Ohio University with a certificate in Executive Leadership from Cornell University.

AHAthat®

THiNKaha has created AHAthat for you to share content from this book.

- ➲ Share each AHA message socially:
  https://aha.pub/HireSmarterSellMore
- ➲ Share additional content: **https://AHAthat.com**
- ➲ Info on authoring: **https://AHAthat.com/Author**

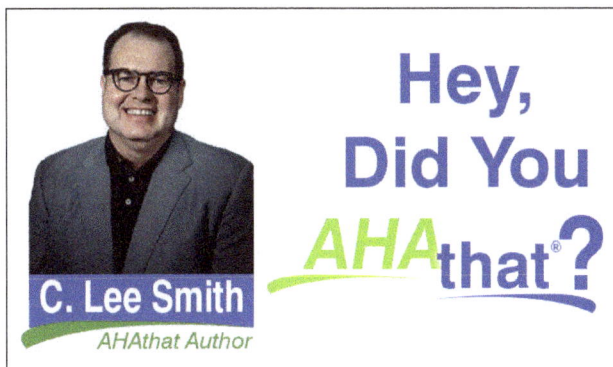

Hey, Did You AHAthat®?

C. Lee Smith

AHAthat Author

www.ingramcontent.com/pod-product-compliance
Lightning Source LLC
Chambersburg PA
CBHW042117190326
41519CB00030B/7530